America is...

for the Graces
A special thank-you to Ayars Borden, who encouraged me
to write a book about America
—L. B.

for Gramps, with love
—S. S.

Also by Louise Borden

The Day Eddie Met the Author
illustrated by Adam Gustavson

Fly High! The Story of Bessie Coleman
co-authored by Mary Kay Kroeger
illustrated by Teresa Flavin

Sleds on Boston Common:
A Story from the American Revolution
illustrated by Robert Andrew Parker

Good Luck, Mrs. K!
illustrated by Adam Gustavson

Good-bye, Charles Lindbergh
illustrated by Thomas B. Allen

The Little Ships:
The Heroic Rescue at Dunkirk in World War II
illustrated by Michael Foreman

ALADDIN PAPERBACKS
An imprint of Simon & Schuster Children's Publishing Division
1230 Avenue of the Americas, New York, NY 10020
Text copyright © 2002 by Louise Borden
Illustrations copyright © 2002 by Stacey Schuett
ALADDIN PAPERBACKS and colophon are registered trademarks of Simon & Schuster, Inc.
Also available in a McElderry hardcover edition.
Designed by Abelardo Martínez
The text of this book was set in Caslon.
Manufactured in China
First Aladdin Paperbacks edition June 2005
4 6 8 10 9 7 5 3
The Library of Congress has cataloged the hardcover edition as follows:
Borden, Louise.
America is . . . /by Louise Borden; illustrated by Stacey Schuett.
p. cm.
ISBN 0-689-83900-6
1. America—Juvenile poetry. 2. United States—Juvenile poetry.
3. Children's poetry, American. [1. United States—Poetry. 2. American poetry.]
I. Schuett, Stacey, ill. II. Title.
PS3352.0696 A83 2002
811'.54—dc21
00-028372
ISBN 1-4169-0286-4 (pbk.)

America is...

BY **LOUISE BORDEN**

ILLUSTRATED BY **STACEY SCHUETT**

ALADDIN PAPERBACKS
New York   London   Toronto   Sydney

America is our country.
It is the place we call home.

We are the nation
whose name means freedom

to people all over the world.

America is . . .

fifty states
from the Atlantic coast
to the Pacific Ocean
and beyond.
The United States
    of America.

Some states are big.
Some states are small.
Thirteen of the states
are very old.

The rest came later,
one by one.

NEW HAMPSHIRE
VERMONT
MAINE
NORTH DAKOTA
MINNESOTA
WISCONSIN
MICHIGAN
NEW YORK
MASSACHUSETTS
RHODE ISLAND
SOUTH DAKOTA
CONNECTICUT
PENNSYLVANIA
IOWA
NEBRASKA
NEW JERSEY
OHIO
INDIANA
MARYLAND
ILLINOIS
WEST VIRGINIA
DELAWARE
WASHINGTON, D.C.
KANSAS
VIRGINIA
KENTUCKY
MISSOURI
NORTH CAROLINA
TENNESSEE
OKLAHOMA
ARKANSAS
SOUTH CAROLINA
MISSISSIPPI
GEORGIA
ALABAMA
TEXAS
LOUISIANA
FLORIDA

America is . . .

a flag of stars and stripes.
Fifty stars for the fifty states we have now.
Thirteen stripes for the thirteen states
that began our nation.

America is the pledge we say at school.

"I pledge allegiance to the flag
of the United States of America
and to the Republic for which it stands,
one Nation, under God, indivisible,
with liberty and justice for all."

It is the song
we sing,
hands over our
hearts:

"Oh, say,
  can you see, by
  the dawn's early light,
What so proudly we hail'd
  at the twilight's last gleaming?
Whose broad stripes and bright stars,
  thro' the perilous fight,
O'er the ramparts we watch'd, were so gallantly
  streaming?
And the rockets' red glare, the bombs bursting in air,
Gave proof thro' the night
that our flag was still there.
Oh say does that star-spangled banner yet wave
O'er the land of the free and the home of the brave?"

America is . . .

old barns
and country roads,
fields of corn
and wheat,

and farmers who work
sunup to sundown.

American farmers grow food
that feeds families
all over the world.

America is . . .

teachers and their students
in schools in every state.
And miners and factory workers,
artists and musicians,
bakers and bankers.
And millions of other people
who work at many different kinds of jobs
at every hour of the day and night.

America is skyscrapers,

tall, with many windows,

up,

up,

up.

And people in cities
who rush to and from work . . .

in cars,
in buses,
in taxicabs,
on subways
and fast trains . . .

WHOOSH!

Honk! Honk!

Hurry! Hurry!

From New York City
to Chicago
to Los Angeles . . .
this is America.

America is . . .

the swamps and bayous
of the Deep South.

And ponds that glimmer
from east to west.

And lakes so huge and deep,
they seem as big as an ocean.

And rushing streams,
and creeks,
and brooks.

And rivers that are long and wide,
that bring our states together
as one vast land
from the Hudson
to the Ohio
to the Mississippi
to the Columbia . . .
this is America.

America is home
to its very first people:

the proud tribes
who live in peace
with the earth
and the sky,
whose words bring wisdom
to all who listen.

And America is those of us who came later:

many kinds of people
from many countries of the world.
We are one family,
and one team.

We are Americans.

And America is . . .

the prairie:

tall grass,
and wind,
and stars.

Listen.

This is America.

America is . . .

the stone walls
of New England,
the forests of the Northwest,
the osprey
and oysters
of the Chesapeake Bay,

and Minnesota winters,
10 degrees below zero
and sometimes colder.

The West and its ranches
are a part of this nation
too.

With
ten-gallon hats
and boots and spurs.
With herds of cattle
and lassos in cowboys' hands.

Rodeo!
Yippee-yei-yay!

This is America.

America is . . .

rugged mountains
with caps of snow

and deserts
that are hot and dry—
110 degrees in the shade.

It is Niagara Falls,
the Grand Canyon,
and sandy beaches
to fly a kite on,
or dig all the way to China.
So much to see
in every state.

America.

America is . . .

big trucks
and wide horizons,
and roads that take us
east and west,
north and south.

And America is
old towns with old names,
and new towns yet to be,
that tell our history,
then and now.

It is a nation
where fifty states meet,
where we are all one.

America is . . .

the land where we are free.

To live.
To speak out.
To worship.
To work.
To play.
To follow our dreams.

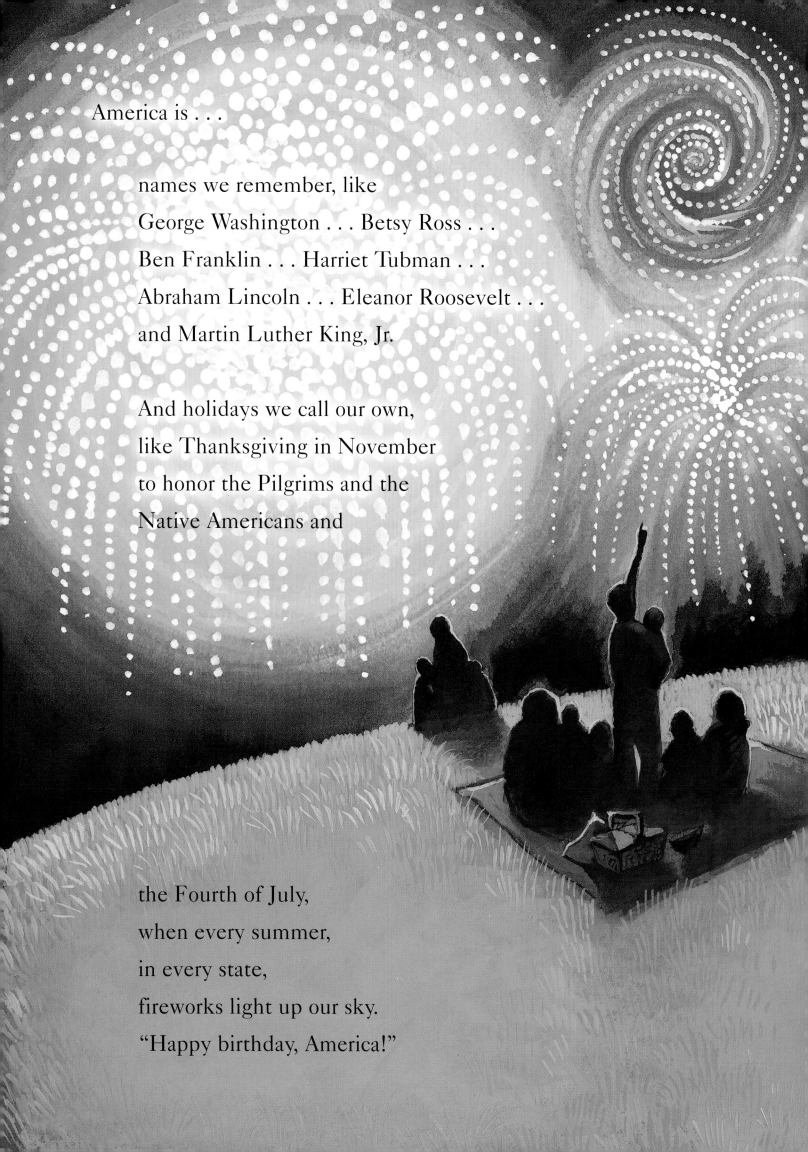

America is . . .

names we remember, like
George Washington . . . Betsy Ross . . .
Ben Franklin . . . Harriet Tubman . . .
Abraham Lincoln . . . Eleanor Roosevelt . . .
and Martin Luther King, Jr.

And holidays we call our own,
like Thanksgiving in November
to honor the Pilgrims and the
Native Americans and

the Fourth of July,
when every summer,
in every state,
fireworks light up our sky.
"Happy birthday, America!"

America is . . .

letters and phone calls,
E-mails and faxes
from family,
from friends,
from the fifty states,
near and far.
Vacations.
And reunions.

We connect
across the rivers,
across the mountains,
across the miles.
Across America.

America is . . .

the stories of *all* of us,
told together.

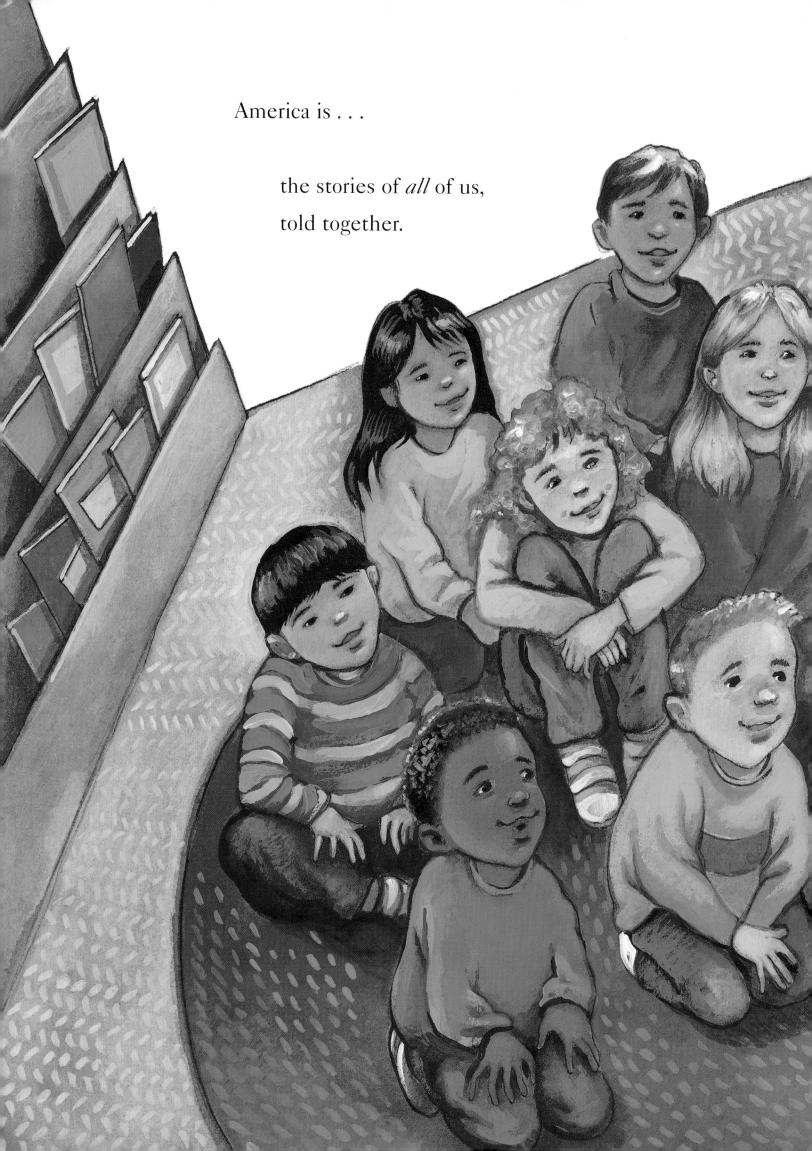

From continent to continent
across the world,
we are the nation
whose name means freedom.

America is our country.

It is the place we call home.